Fireproof

By Naomi Espinoza

Copyright Page

Dedication

This book is dedicated to the greatest Intercessor: Jesus Christ.

For His life of prayer, for bringing the Kingdom of Heaven to the earth, and for leaving us an eternal legacy of intercession that transforms generations.

I dedicate this to every intercessor who has paid a price alongside me in the early hours of the morning, believing for the supernatural move of God over our lives and over our city. Every tear, every groan, and every cry has not been in vain.

I dedicate this to the women who have chosen to rise as intercessors and as helpmates in their homes, restoring the priesthood and establishing God's original design in these times.

And finally, I dedicate this to my children. You have been my greatest motivation to grow, to move forward, and to make a way. May this legacy prepare the path for you and for the generations that will come after you.

Acknowledgments

I would like to express my deepest gratitude to my parents, who gave me the example of parental love and planted in me principles that sustain my life today.

I am grateful to my spiritual father, Apostle Guillermo Maldonado, for his covering, teaching, and example of faith. His impartation has been a foundational part of my spiritual formation.

I give special thanks to my husband, Apostle Victor Espinoza, for his love, his covering, and his faithful walk by my side. Thank you for being a voice of direction, for encouraging me to move forward in God's purpose, and for carrying, together with me, the calling He has entrusted to us.

To every leader and authority figure who contributed to my process of character and maturity—every correction, every piece of counsel, and every word became an instrument in God's hands to shape my life.

And finally, to every intercessor of the early hours who labored in the Spirit for this book—you did not just pray for pages; you prayed for generations.

Thank you.

How to use this Book

Each chapter is designed to lead you through a process:

- Restoring your identity
- Healing through the fire
- Activating your spiritual authority
- Raising up generations
- Establishing the Kingdom in your home

I encourage you not to rush through it. Allow each chapter to minister to your heart. Highlight, write, pray, and return to the sections that speak most deeply to your spirit.

In the chapter *"The Prayers of a Mother,"* you will find space to write. Use it. Declare out loud. Intercede by name. Let this book become a personal altar.

You can use this book:

- As a personal devotional
- As a study resource for women's groups
- As a family prayer guide
- As an activation tool for retreats or conferences

Do not just seek information—seek transformation.

May every page remind you of who you are. May every declaration activate your faith. And may every prayer impact your generations.

This is not the end of your story.

It is the beginning of a woman who is fireproof.

Table of Contents

Introduction

"Who can find a virtuous woman? For her worth is far above rubies." (Proverbs 31:10)

From the beginning, woman was created with purpose, dignity, and value. She was not formed by accident or as an inferior counterpart, but as an essential part of God's perfect design. She was created with femininity, sensitivity, strength, and the capacity to give life—to build and to reflect on the earth the image and likeness of her Creator.

Yet over time, many women have been wounded, confused, and stripped of their identity. Circumstances, betrayal, injustice, and the pressures of society have distorted the way a woman sees herself. What God designed with honor, the world has burdened with pain.

Perhaps you have felt that you've lost your worth. Perhaps life's battles have caused you to forget who you are. But God's original design has not changed. His intention for woman remains intact.

Man and woman were created with distinct functions, yet with equal importance within God's divine plan. When a woman tries to survive outside of that design, she often finds herself exhausted, wounded, or confused. But when she returns to her original purpose, she discovers identity, strength, and direction.

This book was written with a clear purpose: to help you recover, heal, and restore the design for which you were created. No matter how deep the fire you have walked through, God is still forming women who are courageous, restored, and victorious.

Prayer

Beloved Father,

In the beginning, You created the heavens and the earth, and today we return to You as our origin and our Creator. Thank You for forming us intentionally in Your image, with beauty, care, and purpose as women. Restore our identity in every place where it has been shaped by something that did not come from Your voice. Teach us to see ourselves the way You see us.

Lord, You said that it was not good for man to be alone, and You created woman as a suitable helper—necessary within Your original design. Forgive us for allowing that design to be distorted. Heal every misunderstanding and give us the confidence to walk in the purpose You have given us, with wisdom and grace.

Even after the fall, You called the woman "Eve," a life-giver. Thank You that our purpose was never removed. Restore what was broken and awaken within us the life we were created to carry.

I declare that we are created in Your image, chosen and called with purpose. We are life-givers, and we carry life into our homes, our communities, and every place You send us.

In the name of Jesus, Amen.

— Pastora Jovanna Espinoza

CHAPTER 1

Design and Purpose: Returning to the Origin

"In the beginning God created the heavens and the earth."
(Genesis 1:1)

Everything God created, He created with intention. Nothing was the product of chance. Purpose is the original intention for which something was designed, and there is nothing more transformative than a woman knowing and understanding the reason for which she was created.

When humanity invents something, it is to meet a need. The light bulb was created to illuminate darkness, the telephone to connect people across distance. Every creation responds to a specific purpose. In the same way, when God created mankind, He did so with an eternal design, not a temporary one.

"Then God said, 'Let Us make man in Our image, according to Our likeness...'" (Genesis 1:26–27)

Man and woman were created to reflect the image of God on the earth and to exercise dominion under His authority. They were not designed to compete with one another, but to walk in unity, reflecting the character of their Creator. The original purpose only functions when there is alignment with the Creator's design.

Identity Before Function

It is only through identity that a person can understand their purpose. Identity is the truth about who someone is. When a person knows their identity, they find direction, stability, and destiny. The problem is not the absence of purpose, but the absence of revelation of identity.

From the beginning, God gave clear instructions that revealed purpose:

- Be fruitful

- Multiply

- Fill the earth

- Subdue it

- Exercise dominion

- Tend

- Keep

These instructions were not burdens; they were privileges. They were evidence of divine trust. God did not give responsibility to oppress humanity, but to position them.

The Design of Woman

"And the Lord God said, 'It is not good that man should be alone; I will make him a helper comparable to him.'" (Genesis 2:18)

The word "comparable" means suitable, corresponding, complementary. Woman was not created to be inferior or superior, but to complete the design God had established. She was designed as a divine response to a need that man, on his own, could not fulfill.

"And Adam called his wife's name Eve, because she was the mother of all living." (Genesis 3:20)

Eve, from the Hebrew *Chavah*, means "life-giver." This reveals that woman was not created only to give biological life, but to impart spiritual, emotional, and generational life. Her design transcends the natural and is established in the eternal. Her womb is an incubator of destiny. Her voice builds generations. Her presence strengthens covenant.

Unity and Design

God's original design included unity. Man and woman walked together under divine authority, functioning as one body in purpose. When that unity is broken, purpose is weakened—not because God canceled it, but because alignment with the original design has been lost.

If today you are facing crisis in your marriage, conflict in your family, or disorientation in your home, it does not mean that purpose has died. It means it needs to be restored. The power of God is manifested when a woman chooses to return to the original design. This is not the time to give up—it is time to return to the origin.

Restoration of the Design

"And I will put enmity between you and the woman, and between your seed and her Seed; He shall bruise your head, and you shall bruise His heel." (Genesis 3:15)

Even after the fall, God spoke restoration. This

reveals an eternal principle: purpose was never canceled. It was affected, but not eliminated. God is still raising up women who understand their identity and align with His design.

Perhaps you have walked through fire. Perhaps you have been wounded. Perhaps you feel that you have lost direction. But the original design of God over your life remains intact. When a woman understands who she is, heaven responds. And when heaven responds, generations are transformed.

Keys to Remember

- You were created with intention, not by accident
- Identity defines purpose
- God's original design has not been canceled
- Returning to the origin restores direction

Prophetic Declaration

Today I declare over your life that you are returning to the original design for which you were created. I declare that you are not an accident, you are not a mistake, and you are not outside of God's plan. You were formed with eternal intention, and you carry divine purpose within you.

I cancel every lie that has distorted your identity, and I silence every voice that has tried to define you outside of the Creator's design. I declare that you are a carrier of the image of God on the earth. You have been called to build, to strengthen, and to give life.

I declare that your home has purpose, your marriage has purpose, and your children have purpose. Even though you have walked through fire, the purpose over your life remains intact. Nothing has been able to cancel what God wrote about you in eternity.

Today you align with heaven. Today you recover your identity. Today the divine design is activated over your life and over your generations.

In the name of Jesus. Amen.

Prayer

Eternal Father,

In the name of Jesus, today we return to You as our Designer. We recognize that in You alone we find identity, purpose, and direction. We renounce every lie that has distorted who we are, and we declare that we return to Your truth.

Lord, where there has been confusion, bring clarity. Where there has been deception, establish Your truth. Where there has been disorder, align our lives according to Your perfect design. Heal our inner being and restore the way we see ourselves, so we may live from the identity You have given us.

Holy Spirit, guide us to walk in communion with You. Align our thoughts, our decisions, and our steps with Your will. Raise us up as women who are steadfast, secure in their design, and committed to Your purpose.

Today we declare that every distortion loses its power, and that Your truth is established within us. We return to the origin and walk in restoration.

In the name of Jesus, Amen.

— Pastora Janet Valenciano

CHAPTER 2

The Crisis of Design

"And when the woman saw that the tree was good for food, that it was pleasant to the eyes, and a tree desirable to make one wise, she took of its fruit and ate. She also gave to her husband with her, and he ate."
(Genesis 3:6)

God did not create humanity to live separated from Him. The original design included communion, authority, and purpose in perfect harmony. Man and woman walked in unity, without shame, without fear, and without internal distortion. There was clarity in identity, security in purpose, and fullness in their relationship with God. Everything was aligned with the order of heaven, and that alignment produced life in every dimension of their existence. There was no confusion, no inner struggle, no need to hide, because humanity knew who they were and where they came from.

That was the original state of humanity: clarity, security, and direction. There were no internal questions because there was an external voice defining all things. Identity was not constructed; it was received. Purpose was not pursued; it was walked in. Everything flowed from connection with God.

However, that design was not immediately destroyed—it was interrupted through a decision. The fall was not simply an isolated mistake; it was a moment that opened the door to a new reality. A reality where humanity began to live disconnected from its origin, attempting to sustain itself without the reference of God. And when humanity disconnects from its Creator, it inevitably loses direction, because identity is not found within oneself, but in the One who designed all things with eternal intention.

And here begins one of the most important truths:

When humanity loses its reference to God, it begins to create its own version of identity. And every identity created outside of God will always be incomplete.

The crisis of design began the moment the voice of God ceased to be the primary authority in the heart of man. It was not the absence of God that caused the fall, but the substitution of His voice for another. The enemy did not come with force, he did not impose or coerce; he approached with subtlety, with a question that seemed innocent but carried a dangerous distortion:

"Has God indeed said…?" (Genesis 3:1)

That question was not seeking information—it was planting doubt. And doubt, when not confronted with truth, becomes the beginning of deviation.

The enemy does not need to completely remove truth; he only needs to alter it. Because a distorted truth produces a distorted identity. And a distorted identity produces decisions that lead away from purpose.

The fall began internally before it ever manifested externally. Eve did not fall in a moment—it was a process. First she listened to a different voice, then considered a new possibility, then allowed desire to grow within her, and finally acted based on that altered perception. This is how all spiritual distortion works: it does not begin with action, it begins with perception. And when perception changes, decisions change.

That is why the enemy works first in the mind. If he can alter what a woman believes about herself, he can alter how she lives, how she decides, and how she positions herself.

When humanity chose to step away from divine instruction, the consequence was not limited to a single act—it produced a deep rupture in every area. The relationship with God was affected, the relationship between man and woman was fractured, and identity began to distort. What was once natural became uncomfortable.

"Then the eyes of both of them were opened, and they knew that they were naked" (Genesis 3:7)

Shame entered as evidence of internal disconnection. Humanity stopped seeing itself through God's design and began to see itself through the fall.

From that moment forward, humanity began to live trying to cover what it never needed to cover before. Because when identity is lost, security is lost.

The woman, who was designed to give life, began to experience pain in the process. The man, who was called to cover and lead from presence, began to shift blame and avoid responsibility. Harmony was replaced with tension, and the home—intended to be a place of life—began to reflect conflict.

What began in the garden is now seen in homes, families, and generations.

The Modern Manifestation of the Crisis

Today, the distortion of design does not just exist—it has intensified. The modern woman faces struggles that do not only affect her environment, but her deepest identity. These realities are not isolated or superficial; they are the reflection of a spiritual battle aimed at weakening what God designed with eternal intention.

Jesus declared it clearly:

"The thief does not come except to steal, and to kill, and to destroy..." (John 10:10)

The enemy continues to operate under this same principle, attacking the woman not only for who she is, but for what she carries. Because when the woman is affected, the home, the family, and generations are affected.

The Pain that Interrupts Design: Abortion

One of the deepest realities facing women today is abortion. Many times, it is not a decision made from clarity, but from pressure, fear, abandonment, or desperation. It is a moment where a woman finds herself alone, facing a decision that leaves marks far beyond the physical.

It is estimated that millions of abortions occur each year worldwide, reflecting not only a social crisis but a deep spiritual wound within women.[1]

Abortion does not only interrupt a natural process; it can leave emotional and spiritual consequences such as guilt, shame, and internal pain that is often unspoken, yet deeply influences identity.

However, it is important to declare this truth:

---

1 According to the World Health Organization (WHO), it is estimated that approximately 73 million induced abortions occur each year worldwide, reflecting a global reality that deeply impacts women's physical, emotional, and social well-being. Source: World Health Organization (WHO), Abortion Care Guideline, 2022.

"Where sin abounded, grace abounded much more" (Romans 5:20)

God does not respond with condemnation, but with restoration. No matter the past, there is always a path to healing.

The Invisible Weight: Depression, Anxiety, and Postpartum

Many women are fighting battles that are unseen. These are internal struggles that may not always have words, yet they carry significant weight in the soul.

Depression, anxiety, and postpartum depression have become increasingly common. It is estimated that approximately 1 in 7 women experiences postpartum depression, affecting emotional well-being during a season that should be filled with joy.[2]

These conditions do not only affect emotions—they affect identity. A woman may begin to question her worth, her capacity, and her purpose.

But the Word declares:

"For God has not given us a spirit of fear, but of power and of love and of a sound mind" (2 Timothy 1:7)

This reveals that although the battle is real, so is God's response.

The Culture of Despair: Suicide

---

2 Various clinical studies indicate that approximately 1 in 7 women experiences postpartum depression, affecting her emotional well-being, her identity, and her ability to adapt during a crucial stage of motherhood Source: American Psychological Association (APA) and Centers for Disease Control and Prevention (CDC).

The rise in suicide among women reflects a deep crisis of hope. When identity is lost, vision fades. And when vision fades, life begins to feel without purpose.

Recent studies show a concerning increase in suicidal thoughts among women, especially among younger generations, revealing a generation internally struggling without clear direction.[3]

But Scripture declares:

"The Lord is near to those who have a broken heart…" *(Psalm 34:18)*

God does not abandon a woman in her pain—He draws near.

Broken Relationships: Domestic Violence

God's design never included abuse, manipulation, or violence. Yet millions of women live under these realities.

It is estimated that 1 in 3 women has experienced physical or emotional violence at some point in her life.[4]

This deeply distorts the perception of love, authority, and self-worth.

But God's model is clear:

---

3 Recent research has shown a significant increase in levels of suicidal ideation among women, especially among adolescents and young adults, reflecting a global mental health crisis. Source: Centers for Disease Control and Prevention (CDC) and National Institute of Mental Health (NIMH).

4 According to the World Health Organization (WHO), approximately 1 in 3 women worldwide has experienced physical or sexual violence at some point in her life, most often by an intimate partner. Source: World Health Organization (WHO), Violence Against Women Prevalence Estimates, 2021.

"Husbands, love your wives, just as Christ also loved the church..." (Ephesians 5:25)

The love of Christ does not wound—it restores.

Wounds that Distort Design

Many of these decisions and experiences are born in moments of vulnerability. Unprocessed pain begins to shape identity. And when identity is shaped by wounds, life is lived from reaction instead of purpose.

The mind becomes a battlefield.

Thoughts of guilt, inadequacy, rejection, and hopelessness begin to take root. And when those thoughts are not confronted with truth, they become strongholds.

But the Word declares:

"For God has not given us a spirit of fear..." (2 Timothy 1:7)

This means what many women are experiencing does not come from God. But it also means there is a way out in Him.

The Distortion of Identity

The enemy's strongest attack is not external—it is internal. His goal is confusion.

"My people are destroyed for lack of knowledge..." (Hosea 4:6)

A woman without identity will try to define herself by what she has experienced, what others have said, or what the world establishes.

And in that process, many have learned to survive:

They have learned to defend themselves.

They have learned not to depend.

They have learned to build an external strength.

But that strength does not heal—it only protects.

And what began as protection can become distortion.

Design, Not Competition

God did not create man and woman to compete, but to complement one another.

"Male and female He created them" (Genesis 1:27)

Neither is greater nor lesser—both are necessary.

When this design is lost, struggle begins. When it is restored, unity begins.

The Path to Restoration

Despite the crisis, God is still restoring.

"I will restore health to you…" (Jeremiah 30:17)

Restoration begins when a woman returns to God—not to rebuild herself through effort, but to realign with the original design.

Keys to Remember

- The crisis began with a distortion of truth
- The enemy attacks identity to affect generations
- Wounds do not define purpose

- Restoration begins by returning to God

Prophetic Declaration

Today I declare that every distortion loses its power over your life.

I declare that every wound is healed, every lie is silenced, and the truth of God is established in your identity.

You rise with clarity, purpose, and spiritual authority.

In the name of Jesus. Amen.

Prayer

Beloved Father,

Today I declare over every woman reading this book that she has been chosen from before the foundation of the world. I declare that she recognizes that she is a life-giver, formed by Your hands for such a time as this.

Even in the midst of fire, crisis, and pain, Your presence intensifies within her. You strengthen her and raise her up as an instrument to give life, to multiply, and to establish Your purpose on the earth.

I declare that though she walks through the fire, she will not be consumed. As Your Word says: "When you walk through the fire, you shall not be burned..." (Isaiah 43:2). In the midst of the trial, she will be strengthened and established by You.

I prophesy that she will give birth to purpose, raise up generations, and walk in her calling.

You are her keeper and her Savior.

In the name of Jesus, Amen.

— Pastora María Hernández

CHAPTER 3

A Life-Giver in the Midst of the Fire

But what happens when a woman who is called to give life feels empty inside? What happens when the one who was designed to build finds herself broken, and when the one who carries purpose begins to carry pain?

From the beginning, woman was designed as *Chavah*, a life-giver. Her nature was not only biological, but spiritual—to produce, to nurture, to form, and to establish purpose on the earth. Yet the life she was called to manifest does not always develop without opposition. Where there is purpose, there is resistance; and where there is destiny, there is warfare.

Many times, that battle does not begin externally, but within the soul.

Throughout life, there are pains that cannot be seen, yet weigh deeply. Wounds that do not bleed, yet leave internal marks. Processes where no one applauds, yet God is working quietly. In those moments, a woman may begin to question her worth, her purpose, and even her identity.

The story of Hannah reflects this reality with

powerful clarity. Scripture tells us that Peninnah, her rival, provoked her constantly, bringing her into deep distress:

"So it was, year by year… she provoked her; therefore she wept and did not eat." (1 Samuel 1:6–7)

Hannah had position, she had a covenant, and she had a place within her home—but she had no fruit. And in her barrenness, she was emotionally exposed. The problem was not only her condition, but the constant pressure surrounding that condition.

Untreated pain never remains static. It begins as sorrow, develops into frustration, and if it is not brought before God, it can become bitterness. Bitterness is one of the most dangerous conditions of the heart, because it distorts perception, hardens the spirit, and weakens faith. A woman may continue moving forward in life, yet stop expecting anything good. She may continue fulfilling responsibilities, yet carry no hope within.

A wounded woman begins to react instead of respond. She withdraws emotionally, loses spiritual sensitivity, compares herself constantly, and without realizing it, begins to normalize pain as part of her identity. This is the most critical point—when pain is no longer a season, but becomes a way of living.

But Hannah made a different decision.

She did not deny her pain, but she also did not remain in it. Scripture declares that in the midst of her anguish, she began to pray and pour herself out before God:

"And she was in bitterness of soul, and prayed to the Lord and wept in anguish." (1 Samuel 1:10)

Hannah took her pain to the right place. She did

not release it on people, nor did she allow it to become resentment—she transformed it into intercession.

There is a significant difference between expressing pain and surrendering it. Tears may release emotion, but prayer transforms a life. Hannah moved from complaint to crying out, from frustration to surrender, and from pain into covenant with God.

In that moment, her story began to change.

Hannah did not only pray—she committed. Her request was not based solely on her need, but on purpose:

"If You will indeed… give Your maidservant a male child, then I will give him to the Lord…" (1 Samuel 1:11)

This is the point where the heart matures spiritually. It is no longer about receiving alone, but about participating in what God desires to do.

God did not simply answer Hannah—He gave her Samuel. He was not just a son; he was a prophet, an instrument who would impact an entire generation. This reveals a powerful principle: when pain is processed correctly, it does not destroy purpose—it reveals it.

The fire of process has a specific function. It does not come to destroy, but to purify and reveal what truly exists within. Under pressure, faith is revealed, character is formed, and dependence on God becomes evident. This is why many of the greatest stories in Scripture are born in the context of difficulty. There would be no Samuel without Peninnah, no David without Goliath, no Esther without Haman. Pressure is not a sign of abandonment—it is evidence of purpose.

From the beginning, God established that there would be a battle over the seed:

> *"And I will put enmity between you and the woman...*
> *He shall bruise your head..." (Genesis 3:15)*

This declaration reveals that there is a spiritual war over generations. It is not only about children, but about legacy, purpose, and destiny.

Your children are not an accident. The Word declares:

> *"All the days fashioned for me were written in Your*
> *book..." (Psalm 139:16)*

Every life is designed with divine intention. Every generation carries a purpose assigned by God. That is why what heaven establishes, the enemy attempts to resist.

Yet God has not changed His design. He did not create humanity to live limited to the natural. The original design included communion, authority, and a life in His presence. But when humanity fell, it began to seek natural solutions for spiritual problems—and that is where many struggles intensify.

God is calling woman back to her place of origin: His presence. The prophet Joel declares:

> *"And it shall come to pass afterward that I will pour out*
> *My Spirit on all flesh..." (Joel 2:28)*

This includes generations. Your children are not destined to be lost—they are destined to walk in the supernatural. Your home was not designed for chaos, but to reflect the order of heaven.

Healing begins when a woman recognizes her wound, decides not to live from it, brings it before God, forgives, and chooses to believe again. Healing does not mean forgetting—it means no longer bleeding from the same wound. It is allowing God to close what pain once left open.

In conclusion, the fire a woman walks through is not a sign of destruction, but of formation. God does not cancel purpose because of pain—He refines it through it. What once appeared to be an obstacle becomes the very place where purpose is revealed.

Keys to Remember

- Pain does not cancel purpose—it reveals it
- Fire does not destroy—it forms
- What you surrender to God is transformed
- Your process carries an eternal outcome

Prophetic Declaration

Today I declare over your life that the fire you walked through did not destroy you—it formed you. I declare that every wound that tried to define you loses its authority in this moment.

I declare that where there was barrenness, God brings fruit; where there was pain, God raises purpose; and where there were tears, God establishes legacy.

Your generations are covered by covenant. Your children will walk in purpose, and your home will be established according to heaven's design.

I declare that you return to the supernatural realm, that your faith rises, and that your authority is activated.

The fire does not consume you—it refines you.

In the name of Jesus. Amen.

Prayer

Father,

In this moment, I lift up every woman reading this book before You. I pray for a divine restoration of her identity. Where the enemy has spoken lies, where the world has declared that she is not enough, and where confusion has tried to take root, today I rebuke every lie and tear down every label that has been placed over her life, in the name of Jesus.

I declare that every false identity falls now. Her past does not define her. She is who You say she is. She is seated with Christ in a place of authority and belonging.

From this day forward, she stands firm in her position in Christ. She rises with confidence, knowing that she has been called, chosen, and made complete in You. Her identity is restored and remains firmly established in Your truth.

"And you are complete in Him…" (Colossians 2:10)

In the mighty name of Jesus, Amen.

— Pastora Janet Valenciano

The Woman of Today: Restoring Her Identity

Every woman, at some point in her life, is confronted with questions that cannot be ignored. These are not superficial or temporary questions; they arise from the deepest place within the soul and shape the course of her life: *Who am I? Why am I here? What is my purpose?* These questions do not appear by accident. They are evidence of an internal search for something greater—something eternal, something that goes beyond what is visible.

A woman may have clear goals, defined dreams, and still feel that something is missing. She may move forward, achieve goals, fulfill responsibilities, and be recognized externally, yet internally experience a void that nothing material can fill. That void is not weakness—it is a sign that the soul was designed for something deeper than human success. It was designed for connection with God. And until that connection is aligned, there will always be a sense of incompleteness.

From the beginning, God established the design of woman with divine intention. Woman was not created as an afterthought or as a secondary addition within God's plan. She was part of the original design.

"I will make him a helper comparable to him." (Genesis 2:18)

This declaration does not speak of inferiority, but of purpose. The word *comparable* implies correspondence, perfect complement, a help aligned with God's design.

God took from the side of man, from the place closest to the heart, to form woman. This detail is not merely symbolic—it is deeply revealing. Woman was not created from a distance, nor from a position of inferiority or superiority, but from proximity. She was designed to walk in unity, in connection, in shared purpose. Her origin reveals her function: she was not created to compete, but to complete God's design on the earth.

The name Eve means "life-giver." Her identity was directly connected to her purpose. She did not have to discover who she was; she had already been defined by God from the beginning. Her essence was aligned with her assignment. And this reveals an important spiritual principle: when identity is clear, purpose flows naturally.

When Identity Becomes Distorted

The fall did not only introduce pain into humanity—it introduced confusion. From that moment on, human identity was affected, and woman began to search for her value in places that were never designed to sustain her. Disconnection from God produced internal disconnection, and that disconnection gave birth to insecurity, comparison, and a constant need for validation.

Some women seek identity through the acceptance of others, attempting to fill the void through recognition. Others seek control, believing that by managing their environment they will find security. Others develop independence as a defense mechanism against pain, building walls that isolate them more than they protect them. Yet none of these responses can replace what only God can establish.

Identity is not built through human effort. It is not achieved through performance, nor defined by experiences. Identity is received through divine revelation. And while a woman tries to construct her identity apart from God, she will always end up exhausted, frustrated, and empty. But when she receives it in the presence of God, she finds rest. She stops striving to become, and begins to live from who she already is.

The Woman of Today Lives from Redemption

In Christ, a woman does not live under condemnation, but under restoration. Redemption does not only cleanse the past—it completely redefines the present.

"Therefore, if anyone is in Christ, he is a new creation; old things have passed away; behold, all things have become new." (2 Corinthians 5:17)

This truth is not emotional—it is spiritual. It does not depend on how a person feels, but on what God has established.

The woman of today is not defined by her history, her mistakes, her wounds, or her marital status. She is defined by what God says about her. Her identity does not change with circumstances, because it is anchored in an eternal truth. She understands that her value does not come from what she has, what she has achieved, or what others think. Her value comes from her origin: she was created by God and for God.

To live from redemption means to stop looking back for identity in what once was, and to begin walking forward from what God has declared. It means to stop justifying wounds and begin allowing God to heal them. It means to stop living from reaction and begin living from revelation.

Characteristics of the Woman of Today

The woman of today has gone through processes, but she is not defined by them. She has been formed, confronted, healed, and affirmed in her identity—and this is reflected in the way she lives. It is not a theory; it is a visible manifestation.

The woman of today knows her identity in Christ and lives from the presence of God. She does not compete, because she understands that her value is not found in comparison. She does not control, because she has learned to trust God. She does not react from wounds, but responds from the maturity that her process has produced. She builds generations with intention, understanding that her life impacts not only her present, but also her future.

Her strength is not aggressive—it is steady. Her authority is not loud—it is spiritual. She does not need to impose herself to be recognized, because she knows who she is. And when a woman knows who she is, she does not need to constantly prove it. Her security does not come from the outside, but from within—from an identity established by God.

"Charm is deceitful and beauty is passing, but a woman who fears the Lord, she shall be praised." (Proverbs 31:30)

The fear of the Lord becomes the foundation of her life. She does not live to please people, but to honor God. And when her life is aligned with that reverence, everything else finds its proper place.

Returning to the Origin

God's original design was never canceled. It was affected by the fall, but restored through redemption. This means there is always a way back. No matter how far someone has gone, there is always an opportunity to return to God's original design.

Returning to the origin is not going backward—it is realigning with divine intention. It is returning to the presence of God, where identity is healed, purpose is restored, and truth replaces every lie. It is in that place that the soul finds rest, the mind finds clarity, and the heart is affirmed.

In the presence of God, confusion is cleared, wounds are healed, and identity is established. The woman of today does not live from lack—she lives from fullness. She does not move from fear, but from the spiritual authority that has been entrusted to her.

She is not trying to become something. She walks as one who already is. And when a woman walks from that identity, her life becomes a visible manifestation of God's design on the earth.

Keys to Remember

- Identity is not built—it is received from God
- You are not defined by your past
- The woman of today lives from redemption
- Your value comes from your origin

Prophetic Declaration

Today I declare over your life that you recover your original identity in Christ.

I declare that every label your past tried to place on you loses its authority in this moment. Every word that spoke limitation over your life is canceled.

I declare that you are not defined by wounds, mistakes, or circumstances. You are defined by the eternal design of God.

I declare that your value is restored, your voice is affirmed, and your purpose is reactivated.

You rise as a woman of today—secure in your identity, firm in your calling, and established in your spiritual authority.

In the name of Jesus. Amen.

Prayer

Heavenly Father,

Today I declare over every woman reading these words that she is filled with the Father's vision for her life. I declare that she is found in You, and that in Your presence she discovers her starting point to run the race You have assigned to her.

She is not only a suitable helper or a mother; she is a woman set ablaze by Your fire, moved by Your Spirit—like the wheels the prophet Ezekiel saw, driven by what is eternal (Ezekiel 1:16).

I declare that she steps into the plans of the Kingdom as a key part of Your purpose. From this day forward, she leaves behind the lack of identity, breaks free from isolation, and walks in purpose. She is a woman filled with the dream of God for her life, her family, and her community.

In the name of Jesus, Amen.

— Pastora Linda Venzor

CHAPTER 5

The Woman Behind the Vision

"And He Himself gave some to be apostles, some prophets, some evangelists, and some pastors and teachers."
(Ephesians 4:11)

God's purpose has never been limited by gender. The fivefold ministry was given to the church so that it may fulfill its mission on the earth, and within that design, God has raised both men and women to establish His kingdom.

Woman was not only created to give life in the natural realm, but also to give life in the spiritual realm. When a woman understands God's vision, she stops living for herself and begins to live with an eternal perspective. She no longer measures her life by temporary achievements, but by spiritual impact.

Women Who Made History

Throughout Scripture, we find women who walked in God's vision and left a legacy that still remains today.

In Romans 16, the apostle Paul mentions several women who labored alongside him in the expansion of the gospel: Phoebe, Priscilla, Junia, Mary, Tryphena, Tryphosa, Persis, Julia, Olympas, the sister of Nereus, and the mother of Rufus.

These women were not spectators—they were co-laborers.

> *"...they labored with me in the gospel..." (Philippians 4:3)*

This reveals an important principle: the vision of the kingdom is always built in partnership. God does not raise isolated individuals; He raises aligned bodies.

The Apostolic Calling

In the second letter of John, the apostle addresses the "elect lady." In the Greek, *eklektē kuria*, meaning "chosen woman."

> *"The Elder, to the elect lady and her children, whom I love in truth..." (2 John 1:1)*

> *"I rejoiced greatly that I have found some of your children walking in truth..." (2 John 1:4)*

While some interpret this expression symbolically, the language reveals leadership, spiritual responsibility, and authority. This is not a passive figure, but someone who influences, leads, and guards the truth.

God continues to raise women who establish, shepherd, form spiritual children, and steward what He has entrusted to them. Vision requires structure, and structure requires leadership.

The Prophetic Calling

Deborah led as both judge and prophetess in Israel, guiding the people in a time of crisis.

> *"Now Deborah, a prophetess... was judging Israel at that time." (Judges 4:4)*

"…until I, Deborah, arose, arose a mother in Israel." *(Judges 5:7)*

Huldah spoke the word of the Lord at a decisive moment for the nation.

"Then Hilkiah the priest… went to Huldah the prophetess… and she spoke to them, saying, 'Thus says the Lord God of Israel…'" *(2 Kings 22:14–15)*

Anna, in the temple, recognized the Messiah and proclaimed redemption.

"Now there was one, Anna, a prophetess… she did not depart from the temple, but served God with fasting and prayers night and day… and spoke of Him to all those who looked for redemption…" *(Luke 2:36–38)*

None of these women were raised up by accident. Each one responded to a calling.

When a woman lives in the presence of God, her voice is no longer common—it becomes an instrument of divine direction. She does not speak from opinion, but from revelation.

The Evangelistic Calling

The Samaritan woman had an encounter with Jesus that transformed her life, and that encounter became a testimony.

"And many of the Samaritans of that city believed in Him because of the word of the woman…" *(John 4:39)*

She had no title and no recognition, but she had a real encounter with God—and that was enough to impact an entire city.

When a woman has a genuine encounter with Christ, she cannot remain silent. Her life becomes a message that others can see and believe.

The Pastoral Heart

In the parable of the lost coin:

"Or what woman, having ten silver coins, if she loses one coin, does not light a lamp, sweep the house, and search carefully until she finds it? … Likewise, I say to you, there is joy in the presence of the angels of God over one sinner who repents." (Luke 15:8–10)

Jesus presents the image of a woman who searches diligently for what has been lost.

This scene reveals the pastoral heart:

- Compassion for what is lost
- Care for what belongs
- Perseverance until it is found.

The pastoral heart is not satisfied with what is present—it focuses on what is missing. It does not rest until what has value in the kingdom is restored.

Women Who Sustain the Vision

Lydia, a businesswoman, played a key role in establishing the apostolic work in Philippi. Her generosity and willingness opened doors for the expansion of the gospel.

In the same way, during Jesus' ministry, we find women who supported the work with their resources:

"…certain women who had been healed… Mary called

Magdalene… Joanna… Susanna, and many others who provided for Him from their substance." (Luke 8:1–3)

This shows us that vision is not only preached—it is sustained.

The woman behind the vision does not only participate—she invests. She does not only listen—she builds. She understands that what God has given her is not just for her benefit, but for the advancement of the kingdom.

The Woman Behind the Vision

The woman who walks in vision understands her place in the purpose of God. She is not distracted or disoriented, she is aligned.

- She understands her calling
- She works in unity
- She lives with eternal purpose
- She sustains the work of God
- She forms spiritual generations
- She does not seek recognition—she seeks fulfillment

She does not need recognition to move forward, because her motivation is not to be seen, but to be obedient. Her focus is not to stand out, but to make an impact.

Conclusion

God is still raising women who walk in His vision— women who establish, prophesy, evangelize, shepherd, and build.

- The story did not end with Deborah.
- It did not end with Junia.
- It did not end with the Samaritan woman.

The story continues.

And it continues with you.

Keys to Remember

- God calls women to actively participate in His work
- Vision is built in unity
- Your life carries a spiritual assignment
- You were not called to observe, but to build

Prophetic Declaration

Today I declare over your life that you will not only know your identity, but also your assignment.

I declare that God activates in you an unobstructed vision and an eternal purpose that will not be stopped.

I declare that your voice will be an instrument of direction, your faith will be an example, and your life will be a platform to establish the kingdom of God on the earth.

You will walk in unity, work in partnership, and raise spiritual generations that reflect the glory of God.

You will not be a spectator in this generation—you will be an active participant in the vision of God.

You rise as a woman behind the vision.

In the name of Jesus. Amen.

Prayer

Lord,

Today we lift our voices, recognizing the calling You have placed upon the intercessory woman. I declare that she is a woman who does not retreat, who does not give up, and who does not negotiate her spiritual assignment. Thank You for those who rise in the secret place, who carry what is unseen, and who remain steadfast in the midst of the battle.

I declare in the name of Jesus that the intercessory woman is strengthened with power in her inner being. Her intercession breaks chains, opens doors, and tears down strongholds. Where others see chaos, she sees an altar; where others see defeat, she sees victory.

Anoint her hands for war and her heart for the battle. Give her discernment to see beyond the natural, courage to stand in the gap, and authority to declare life where there is death.

I declare that her cry moves heaven. When she prays, hell trembles; when she rises, walls fall.

Thank You for the women who sustain generations from the secret place. You hear, you respond, and You move through them.

In the name of Jesus, Amen.

— Pastora Adelita Rodríguez

CHAPTER 6

The Intercessory Woman

"Your kingdom come. Your will be done on earth as it is in heaven."
(Matthew 6:10)

From the beginning, God created humanity to live in His presence. That was the original environment: communion, authority, and purpose. Man was not designed to live separated from God, but in constant connection with Him.

However, through the fall, humanity was expelled from Eden and lost that direct access. What was once natural became distant. But when Jesus came to the earth, He did not come only to save souls—He came to restore access to the Father.

Through Him, heaven became available once again.

Prayer then becomes the bridge between heaven and earth. It is the means by which what is invisible begins to manifest in the visible.

Prayer as a Lifestyle

The disciples observed the life of Jesus. They saw His miracles, His authority, and His impact. Yet they did not ask Him to teach them how to preach or perform miracles.

They said:

"Lord, teach us to pray." (Luke 11:1)

They understood something essential: the power of Jesus' ministry did not come from what He did publicly, but from His private life with the Father.

Jesus prayed constantly—early in the morning, throughout the day, and at night:

"He went out to the mountain to pray and continued all night in prayer to God." (Luke 6:12)

Prayer was not an occasional activity; it was His lifestyle.

Prayer is dialogue. Intercession is intervention.

To pray is to speak with God. To intercede is to stand before God on behalf of another.

The Power of Intercession

"The effective, fervent prayer of a righteous man avails much." (James 5:16)

Intercession does not manipulate God; it aligns with His will. It is not about convincing God to do something, but about declaring on earth what He has already established in heaven.

When a woman intercedes, she positions herself as a vessel of connection between two realms. She becomes a voice that establishes heaven on earth.

Intercession produces real impact. Through it, processes of:

- Salvation

- Restoration
- Healing
- Freedom
- Direction

are released.

But intercession is not instant. It requires endurance.

When You Don't See Results

One of the greatest challenges in a life of prayer is remaining steadfast when there are no immediate results. Many times, a woman prays—and nothing seems to change.

That is where many stop.

But in the spiritual realm, silence does not mean absence of response. It means process.

God does not respond based only on urgency; He responds according to purpose.

Intercession matures when it stops depending on what is seen and stands firm on what God has spoken.

Four Keys to Effective Intercession

1. Perseverance

"Praying always... being watchful to this end with all perseverance..." (Ephesians 6:18)

Perseverance is remaining even when there is no visible evidence. It is continuing to believe when the result has not yet appeared.

Many answers do not come because God did not

speak—but because prayer stopped too soon.

The testimony of a mother who prays for her child for years reminds us of a powerful truth: time does not cancel the Word of God—perseverance activates it.

2. Love

"...faith working through love." (Galatians 5:6)

Love is the motivation behind intercession.

If we do not love, we do not carry. If we do not carry, we do not intercede.

Jesus interceded because He loved first. His love led Him to identify with humanity and to give Himself completely.

True love moves us beyond ourselves. It leads us to bring before the Father the needs of others as if they were our own.

3. Compassion

"So Jesus had compassion and touched their eyes..." (Matthew 20:34)

Compassion is not pity—it is an active response to pain.

Jesus was moved by compassion. He did not only see the need; He responded to it.

Compassion activates faith. When a woman develops compassion, her prayer moves from being surface-level to becoming a deep cry.

The intercessory woman is not indifferent. She perceives, feels, and responds spiritually.

4. Holiness

"...be holy in all your conduct because it is written, 'Be holy, for I am holy.'" (1 Peter 1:15–16)

An effective intercessor lives in consecration.

Holiness does not mean perfection, but separation for God. It is a continual decision to turn away from sin and live aligned with His will.

Holiness keeps the heart clean and the conscience sensitive to the voice of the Holy Spirit. Without spiritual sensitivity, prayer becomes routine; with sensitivity, it becomes direction.

"The Spirit Himself makes intercession for us..." (Romans 8:26)

This reveals that we are not alone in prayer. The Holy Spirit helps us when we do not know what to say.

Praying with the Spirit and with Understanding

"I will pray with the spirit, and I will also pray with the understanding." (1 Corinthians 14:15)

Praying with understanding means using the Word of God as a foundation—declaring what God has already established.

Praying in the Spirit means surrendering to the guidance of the Holy Spirit, allowing Him to intercede through us according to the perfect will of God.

Both dimensions are necessary. The Word gives us foundation; the Spirit gives us direction.

The Woman Who Manifests the Kingdom

The intercessory woman understands that her battle is not against flesh and blood. She does not fight people—she fights against what seeks to misalign the purpose of God.

She does not war against her husband, her children, or natural circumstances. Her focus is spiritual.

Spiritual warfare does not begin in conflict—it begins in the presence.

Without warfare, there is no victory. But without presence, there is no authority.

Conclusion

The intercessory woman does not live passively—she lives watchfully. She does not react emotionally; she responds spiritually. Her prayer life is not occasional; it is consistent.

She understands that her voice carries weight in heaven and that her intercession has generational impact.

When a woman rises to intercede, heaven responds.

Keys to Remember

- Prayer connects heaven to earth
- Intercession requires perseverance
- Love, compassion, and holiness sustain prayer
- Your voice carries weight in heaven

Prophetic Declaration

Today I declare over your life that your voice in prayer will carry weight in heaven.

I declare that the Holy Spirit activates within you perseverance, love, compassion, and holiness.

I declare that you will not grow weary in interceding for your home, your children, and your generation.

I declare that heaven backs your prayers because they are aligned with the will of God.

You rise as an intercessory woman—steadfast, consistent, and led by the Spirit.

In the name of Jesus, Amen.

Prayer

Heavenly Father,

Today I pray for every woman holding this book in her hands, declaring that she has gone through a process and is now positioned to cross into the next season. Awaken in her a hunger, a determination, and a deep desire to move forward in Your purpose.

I declare that she hears Your voice calling her into deeper places in Your presence. She has come to the threshold of multiplication, growth, and fulfillment. That threshold is maturity.

Awaken within her a longing to grow internally, to develop the character of Christ, and to walk in discipline. Today she leaves behind complacency, procrastination, pain, the past, and every offense, and chooses to walk with You.

I declare that she steps into a new season. She is clothed with self-discipline, order, and wise decisions. She receives a teachable spirit, a moldable heart, and walks in love, joy, and self-control.

In the name of Jesus, Amen.

— Pastora Linda Venzor

CHAPTER 7

The Woman in Her Maturity

"And the rib which the Lord God had taken from man He made into a woman, and He brought her to the man."
(Genesis 2:22)

God formed woman with intention, honor, and purpose. She was not created as an afterthought, but as part of God's eternal design to reflect His image on the earth. From the beginning, her existence was tied to a purpose greater than the natural. She was not designed merely to occupy space, but to manifest the character of God on the earth through her life, her decisions, and her influence.

"And the Lord God formed man of the dust of the ground, and breathed into his nostrils the breath of life..." (Genesis 2:7)

When God breathed life into man, He did not only impart existence—He imparted identity and assignment. And when He formed woman from the side of man, He revealed an eternal principle: woman was designed to walk in unity, with purpose, dignity, and spiritual responsibility. She was not formed from the ground, but from a place of proximity, which speaks of relationship, connection, and shared purpose.

"This is now bone of my bones and flesh of my flesh." (Genesis 2:23)

The original design was not merely functional—it was deeply relational. It was grounded in communion with God, alignment with His will, and constant dependence on His presence. Everything flowed from that connection.

When the Design Is Interrupted

With the fall, that design was affected. It was not eliminated, but it was distorted. Confusion, pain, disorder, and internal struggles entered. The woman, who was created to give life, began to experience loss, frustration, and emotional wounds that affected her identity and the way she related to others.

Throughout history, many women have lived not from design, but from survival. They have learned to react instead of respond, to defend instead of trust, to carry instead of rest.

But God's plan never changed.

Jesus came not only to forgive sin, but to restore the original design. He did not come to create a new identity, but to return humanity to its rightful position before God. Redemption is not an upgrade—it is a complete restoration.

The Model of Jesus: Growth and Maturity

Jesus Himself walked through a process:

"And Jesus increased in wisdom and stature, and in favor with God and men." (Luke 2:52)

This reveals a spiritual principle: maturity does not happen automatically—it is developed. It is the result of walking with God over time, responding to His voice, and allowing Him to form character in every stage of life.

In the same way, God leads a woman through progressive processes that form her completely. These are not titles or visible positions, but internal transformations that produce stability, identity, and spiritual authority. Each stage is not a final destination, but preparation for what comes next.

Stages of Maturity

God works in the life of a woman through processes that lead her into full maturity. These stages are not rigid or identical for everyone, but they reveal spiritual principles every woman is called to develop:

1. Being a daughter

2. Being a woman

3. Being a wife

4. Being a mother

Each stage builds upon the previous one. Authority cannot be sustained without identity, and generations cannot be formed without first being formed.

1. Being a Daughter

The first stage is identity: being a daughter of God. Before exercising authority, before building or leading, a woman must be established as a daughter. Because a daughter knows who she belongs to, and from that security, she can grow without being dominated by wounds or insecurity.

"But as many as received Him… to them He gave the right to become children of God." (John 1:12)

In this stage, a woman learns to depend on God as her Father. She learns to hear His voice, to receive correction with love, and to allow her inner life to be healed in His presence. This is where the lies of abandonment, rejection, and self-sufficiency are broken.

The enemy will always try to introduce a voice of independence: *"Do it on your own," "No one understands you," "No one is there for you."* But a mature daughter responds with conviction: *God is my Father, and in Him I have everything I need.*

Without identity, there is no stability. But when identity is established, life begins to align.

2. Being a Woman

The second stage is responsibility and authority. A mature woman understands that she was created to build, manage, and exercise dominion according to God's design. She does not do this from competition, but from function.

> *"Then God blessed them, and God said to them… have dominion…" (Genesis 1:28)*

Authority is not control—it is alignment. A woman who understands her design does not need to impose herself, because her authority flows from obedience. She learns to walk firmly without losing sensitivity, and to exercise dominion without disconnecting from the heart of God.

At this stage, she stops reacting emotionally and begins responding spiritually. She understands that her influence does not come from outward strength, but from inward alignment.

The key to authority is consistent obedience.

3. Being a Wife

The third stage is covenant. Here, a woman learns to walk in unity, to build alongside her husband, and to reflect the design of Christ and the Church. It is not a relationship based on control or dominance, but on purpose, honor, and mutual growth.

"For this reason a man shall leave his father and mother and be joined to his wife…" (Ephesians 5:31)

Marriage, under God's design, does not simply unite two people—it forms character, purifies intentions, and reveals areas that need transformation. It is a place where grace, forgiveness, and maturity are practiced.

However, clarity must be established:

Honor is not allowing abuse. Submission is not tolerating violence. God's design protects—it does not destroy.

The model of Christ toward the Church is sacrificial love, care, and devotion. That is the standard.

4. Being a Mother

The fourth stage is the reproduction of legacy. Motherhood is not only biological—it is spiritual. It involves forming, nurturing, and establishing purpose in others.

"…but all things are from God." (1 Corinthians 11:12)

"And the things that you have heard from me… commit these to faithful men who will be able to teach others also." (2 Timothy 2:2)

A mature woman understands that her life does not end with her. Her calling is to multiply, to form generations, and to leave a legacy that extends beyond her lifetime. She no longer lives focused only on what she receives, but on what she can impart.

Her home, her children, her disciples—all become ground where God's purpose is planted.

The joy of a mature woman is not only in what she achieves, but in what she establishes in others.

Conclusion

God is calling women to maturity—to return to identity, to walk in spiritual authority, and to raise generations with eternal purpose.

Maturity is not an event. It is a continuous process.

It is not about moving quickly, but about growing correctly. Just as Jesus grew and was formed in every stage, a woman is also led by God through processes that establish her firmly in His design.

And when a woman matures, she does not only transform her life—she transforms generations.

Keys to Remember

- Maturity is a process, not an event
- Identity sustains authority
- God forms a woman through stages
- Your life is designed to multiply

Prophetic Declaration

Today I declare over your life that you are entering a new season of spiritual maturity.

I declare that your identity as a daughter is affirmed and established in the Father. Every voice that tried to confuse you loses its authority over your mind and your heart.

I declare that God activates in you spiritual authority with gentleness, firmness with tenderness, and wisdom to build.

I declare that your home will be aligned with the design of heaven, and that your generations will be protected, formed, and raised in purpose.

I declare that you will not live reacting from wounds, but responding from identity.

And what the enemy intended to use to break you, God will use to form you.

In the name of Jesus. Amen.

Prayer

Beloved Father,

Today I lift my voice before You for every woman who has been marked by absence, rejection, or a lack of identity. I declare that every invisible wound is exposed to the light of Your presence, and every void is filled by the perfect love of the Father.

In the name of Jesus, I declare that every lie that formed a false identity falls now. Every voice that said "you are not enough," "you don't belong," or "you are not loved" loses its authority. Today, truth is established: she is Your daughter.

Father, reveal Yourself as Father—not as an idea, but as a living reality in her heart. Heal every distorted image formed through past experiences and replace it with the truth of who You are: near, faithful, present, and restoring.

I declare that she receives the Spirit of adoption. She no longer lives from abandonment, but from belonging. She no longer seeks approval, because she has been accepted. She no longer walks in insecurity, but in identity.

Today she returns to the origin. Today she aligns with Your voice. Today her identity is restored from the root.

I declare that she rises as a daughter—firm, secure, loved, and positioned in You.

In the name of Jesus. Amen.

— Prophet Naomi Espinoza

CHAPTER 8

Returning to the Father: Restored Daughters

"A father of the fatherless, a defender of widows, is God in His holy habitation."
(Psalm 68:5)

There is a deep need in the heart of a woman that cannot always be explained with words. It is a constant search—sometimes silent, sometimes evident, but always present. It is the need to belong, to be affirmed, to be seen, to be loved correctly. This is not a weakness; it is design. A woman was created to respond to love, to flourish in an environment of identity, covering, and direction.

However, when that need is not properly met, a woman begins to search in the wrong places for what can only be found in God. And it is there that a life marked by emotional lack, insecurity, and internal confusion often begins.

The Invisible Wound

Many women have grown up with voids that are not always visible. Some experienced the physical absence of a father. Others, even with a present father figure, never received affirmation, direction, or emotional covering. Though the circumstances may differ, the result is often the same: a fragmented identity.

The lack of fatherhood does not only leave an emotional void; it creates a constant need for validation. A woman begins to seek approval through relationships, achievements, or external recognition, attempting to fill a space that was never designed to be filled by people.

"Father of the fatherless and a defender of widows, is God in His holy habitation" (Psalm 68:5)

God does not ignore this reality. He is not indifferent to the pain of absence. He reveals Himself precisely as Father to those who have experienced lack.

Many of these wounds do not have a clear starting point; they were formed in silence, in seasons where a woman did not yet have the tools to process what she was living through. They are wounds that are not always remembered with clarity, but they manifest in decisions, reactions, and in the way she perceives herself.

A word never spoken, affirmation never given, a constant absence, repeated rejection—these begin to form an internal narrative. And over time, that narrative becomes a truth to the heart, even if it is not the truth of God.

What makes these wounds so dangerous is that they are not always easily identified. Many women have learned to function, to move forward, and to carry responsibilities—but they do so from a wounded place. And when life is built on an unhealed wound, eventually that wound begins to speak louder than the truth.

This is why healing is not optional—it is necessary. Because what is not healed is transferred. And what is not confronted is repeated.

Seeking Identity in the Wrong Places

When a woman has not been properly affirmed, she begins to build her identity based on what she has experienced. If she was rejected, she sees herself as insufficient. If she was abandoned, she perceives herself as unworthy of being kept. If she was wounded, she learns to protect rather than to open.

Without realizing it, she begins to live from the wound instead of from design.

This often shows up in unstable relationships, emotional dependency, fear of abandonment, or a constant need to prove her value. Not because she lacks value, but because she has not recognized it from the right source.

The truth is clear:

Identity is not built from experience—it is received from the Father.

The Spirit of Adoption

God does not only restore—He redefines.

"For you did not receive the spirit of bondage again to fear, but you received the Spirit of adoption by whom we cry out, 'Abba, Father'" (Romans 8:15)

This means a woman is not destined to live from abandonment, but from adoption. Not from fear, but from belonging.

Being a daughter is not an emotion—it is a position. It is understanding that your identity is not determined by what you received on earth, but by what God established in heaven.

Spiritual adoption does not only change your relationship with God—it changes how you see yourself, how you decide, and how you walk.

The spirit of adoption is not just a doctrine; it is an experience that transforms the entire life of a woman. It is the moment she stops seeing herself as someone trying to fit in and begins to understand that she already belongs. She no longer lives from insecurity, but from the certainty that she has been received.

When a woman receives this revelation, something breaks internally: the need for external approval begins to lose its power. She no longer needs to validate herself through relationships, achievements, or recognition, because she has been affirmed by the Father.

Adoption also redefines how she faces life. A daughter does not live with a scarcity mindset—she lives with an inheritance mindset. She is not trying to survive; she understands there is provision, covering, and backing that flows from her relationship with God.

And it is in this place that true freedom begins. Because a woman who understands she is a daughter stops striving for identity and begins to walk in it.

Healing Identity

Healing does not take place when the wound is ignored, but when it is brought before God. Many women have tried to move forward without processing what they have lived, but what is not healed will always manifest in some area of life.

God does not only want you to move forward—He wants you restored.

"But as many as received Him, to them He gave the right to become children of God…" (John 1:12)

This means identity can be fully restored—not partially, not superficially, but completely.

When a woman understands she is a daughter, she stops begging for what already belongs to her. She stops looking outward for what has already been established within her by God.

Returning to the Father

The process of restoration begins with a decision: to return.

Not returning to the past, but returning to the origin. Returning to the voice that defines, the love that heals, the presence that restores.

"Return to Me, and I will return to you…" (Malachi 3:7)

God is not distant. He is not waiting for perfection—He is waiting for surrender.

Returning to the Father is not a religious act; it is an act of identity.

It is recognizing: "I do not have to keep living from my wound. I can live from truth."

Returning to the Father is not always emotional—many times it is a spiritual decision. It is choosing to draw near even when emotions do not align, even when questions remain unanswered, even when the past still carries weight.

It is an act of faith. It is saying, "Even if I do not understand everything I have lived, I choose to trust who You are."

Many women wait to "feel ready" to return, but

restoration does not begin when you feel ready—it begins when you choose to surrender. And in that surrender, God begins to do what no person could ever do: heal from the root.

Returning to the Father also requires letting go of wrong versions of Him. Many times, the perception of God has been shaped by human experiences. But God is not the reflection of what was missing—He is the restoration of what was never present.

When a woman returns to the Father, she does not only find comfort—she finds identity, direction, and purpose.

Restored Daughters

A restored woman is not one who was never wounded, but one who allowed God to heal what was broken.

She no longer lives seeking approval, because she knows she has already been accepted. She no longer lives with fear of abandonment, because she understands she has never been alone. She no longer defines herself by her past, because she has embraced her identity in Christ.

"Therefore, if anyone is in Christ, he is a new creation..."
(2 Corinthians 5:17)

Being a daughter changes everything.

- It changes how you see yourself.

- It changes how you speak.

- It changes how you walk.

A restored daughter does not live reacting to her

past—she lives responding to truth. Her history is no longer the starting point of her decisions; her identity in God is.

This does not mean she never feels pain again, but pain no longer has authority over her life. It no longer defines her worth or limits her purpose. She has learned to live from a different position.

A restored woman also changes the atmosphere wherever she goes. What was healed in her begins to impact others. The way she loves is different. The way she speaks is different. The way she relates is different.

She no longer tries to fill emptiness in others, because she has been filled. She no longer lives from need, but from fullness.

And this is where restoration becomes legacy. Because a healed woman does not just live differently— she raises different generations.

Conclusion

The absence of fatherhood may leave a mark, but it does not have the final word.

God is still calling daughters. He is still restoring identity. He is still healing hearts.

No matter what was missing on earth—nothing is lacking in God.

Keys to Remember

- Identity is not built—it is received
- The absence of fatherhood may affect, but it does not define
- God reveals Himself as Father to restore identity
- Being a daughter is a position, not an emotion

Prophetic Declaration

Today I declare that every wound of abandonment is healed.

I declare that your identity is restored and that you rise as a daughter—firm, secure, and positioned in God.

You no longer seek approval, because you have been accepted. You no longer walk in fear, because you have a Father.

Today you return to the origin. Today you are restored.

In the name of Jesus. Amen.

Prayer

Eternal Father,

Today I declare over every woman reading these words that she receives revelation of what belongs to her in You. I declare that her spiritual eyes are opened to see that she was not called to live in lack, but in inheritance.

I declare that every limiting mindset breaks now. Every idea that caused her to settle for less, every voice that held her back, and every insecurity that made her doubt loses its power in the name of Jesus.

Just as Achsah asked for the springs, I declare that she receives wisdom to ask for what she needs to establish. Just as the daughters of Zelophehad rose up, I declare that she rises with boldness to claim what belongs to her. Just as the daughters of Job were recognized, I declare that she is affirmed and positioned in her place.

Father, activate in her an inheritance mindset. That she no longer thinks from lack, but from spiritual abundance. That she does not live waiting for permission, but walks in identity.

I declare that she rises as a woman who establishes, builds, and multiplies what You have placed in her life.

Today she claims what has already been given in heaven.

In the name of Jesus. Amen.

— Prophet Naomi Espinoza

CHAPTER 9

The Woman Who Claims her Inheritance

"The daughters of Zelophehad speak what is right. You shall surely give them a possession of inheritance..."
(Numbers 27:7)

There comes a moment in the life of every woman when she stops surviving and begins to take her position. It is the point where she no longer only understands who she is, but begins to walk in what belongs to her. This is not an external shift—it is an internal transformation that redefines how she speaks, how she decides, and how she moves.

Many women have lived waiting for someone else to give them permission to move forward. They have learned to limit themselves, to settle, or to remain silent—not because they lack value, but because they have not recognized what has already been given to them by God. But there comes a moment when that passivity breaks, and a woman realizes she was not only called to receive—she was called to establish.

Inheritance is not something that is begged for—it is something that is recognized.

The Right to Ask: The Courage of Achsah

Scripture presents us with a woman who understood this clearly. Her name was Achsah, the daughter of

Caleb. She had already received a portion of land as her inheritance, yet she understood that what she had, although valuable, was not enough to sustain what God intended to do through her life.

"And it was so, when she came to him, that she persuaded him to ask her father for a field. So she dismounted from her donkey; and Caleb said to her, 'What do you wish?' She answered, 'Give me a blessing; since you have given me land in the South, give me also springs of water.' So he gave her the upper springs and the lower springs." (Joshua 15:18–19)

Achsah was not passive. She did not settle for what she initially received. She understood that land without water could not produce. And she had the courage to ask for what was necessary for her inheritance to bear fruit.

But there is something deeper in this story. Achsah was not thinking only about possession—she was thinking about building. A woman who understands inheritance does not settle for owning—she desires to multiply.

The upper and lower springs were not a small addition; they were the key to productivity. They represented constant provision, sustainability in every season, and the ability to build something that would not depend on external conditions. It was the difference between having land and producing life.

Here we see something powerful: Achsah, together with her husband, received the capacity to establish, to build, and to sustain. They did not just inherit land— they inherited the resources necessary to make it fruitful. This reveals God's design: inheritance is not only to be possessed, it is to be developed.

The name Achsah, in its Hebrew root, is associated

with the idea of "adornment" or "ornament." This reveals something prophetic—she did not just receive an inheritance; she beautified it. She did not settle for occupying space; she gave it value, form, and purpose.

There are women who receive what God gives them but never transform it. And there are others, like Achsah, who take what they receive and turn it into something that reflects the glory of God.

She did not ask out of ambition—she asked out of vision.

She did not ask for more for herself—she asked for what was necessary to establish something that would sustain generations.

Breaking Limits: The Daughters of Zelophehad

Another story that reveals this truth is that of the daughters of Zelophehad. In a culture where inheritance was given only to men, these women chose to rise and speak.

> *"Then came the daughters of Zelophehad… and they stood before Moses… and said: 'Our father died in the wilderness… Why should the name of our father be removed from among his family because he had no son? Give us a possession among our father's brothers.'" (Numbers 27:1–4)*

They did not accept a system that excluded them. They did not rebel with disorder, but neither did they submit to a limitation that was not aligned with the heart of God.

And here we find something significant: their names.

- **Mahlah**—associated with weakness or sickness.

- **Noah**—connected with movement or rest.
- **Hoglah**—linked to dance or celebration.
- **Milcah**—representing royalty or authority.
- **Tirzah**—meaning delight or pleasure.

These names reflect processes, conditions, and realities, yet none of them allowed those conditions to define their destiny. They stood together, positioned themselves with clarity, and spoke with authority.

And they did not only gain the attention of Moses—they gained the attention of God.

> *"And the Lord spoke to Moses, saying: 'The daughters of Zelophehad speak what is right...'" (Numbers 27:6–7)*

This is powerful. God did not just hear them—He validated them.

A woman who understands her identity carries a voice that heaven recognizes.

Their action did not only change their story—it changed a law. It opened a path for future generations. It established justice where limitation once stood.

What they did was not simply claim inheritance—it was to establish a precedent.

A Recognized Inheritance: The Daughters of Job

The story of Job also reveals a restorative principle.

> *"In all the land were found no women so beautiful as the daughters of Job; and their father gave them an inheritance among their brothers." (Job 42:15)*

Scripture mentions their beauty, but it does not stop

there. In God's design, beauty is never the destination—it is only an expression.

A woman in identity is not only one who is seen—she is one who is recognized.

Job did not only see his daughters as beautiful—he saw them as worthy of inheritance. He positioned them, included them, and affirmed them. This breaks the mindset of exclusion and establishes an eternal principle: a woman is not secondary in God's purpose.

A woman in identity does not compete with man—she walks alongside him. She does not seek to replace him—she completes the design.

Here we see the heart of a father. A father who does not limit but affirms. A father who does not exclude but recognizes.

This reflects the heart of God: before Him, identity is not limited by gender but defined by purpose.

An Inheritance Mindset

One of the reasons many women do not walk in what God has given them is because they have not developed an inheritance mindset.

An inheritance mindset is not about receiving things, it is about understanding position.

A woman who does not know she has an inheritance lives as if she has no right. She settles for less, adapts to what she finds, and tolerates what she should never tolerate.

But a woman who understands she is a daughter begins to think differently.

She no longer asks if she can—she asks how to

establish.

She no longer questions if she deserves—she walks in what belongs to her.

She no longer lives limited by her past—she positions herself from the promise.

An inheritance mindset transforms how a woman sees herself. And when her perception changes, her life follows.

Claiming What God Has Already Given

Claiming inheritance is not an act of pride, it is an act of alignment.

It is understanding that there are things God has already established, but that require faith to be activated.

"Blessed be the God and Father… who has blessed us with every spiritual blessing…" (Ephesians 1:3)

This means many of the answers a woman is searching for have already been given but have not yet been recognized.

Not everything God gives manifests automatically. Some things must be walked out. Some must be believed. And others must be claimed.

To claim is not to demand from God—it is to agree with Him.

It is to say: "I will not live by what I see—I will live by what You have spoken."

And when a woman steps into that level of faith, she stops waiting and begins establishing.

Conclusion

The woman who claims her inheritance is not arrogant—she is aware.

She does not live waiting for permission—she lives from identity.

She does not settle for less—she walks in what belongs to her.

Because when a woman understands what belongs to her, she stops surviving and begins to establish.

Keys to Remember

- Inheritance is not begged for—it is recognized
- God validates the voice of a woman aligned with Him
- Identity activates authority
- What is not claimed is not manifested

Prophetic Declaration

Today I declare that you rise with a new revelation of what belongs to you.

I declare that every limiting mindset falls, and you begin to walk in the fullness of what God has established for your life.

I declare that you have the courage to ask, the authority to speak, and the faith to establish.

Today—you claim your inheritance.

In the name of Jesus. Amen.

Prayer

Father, in the name of Jesus,

Today we declare that every woman who reads this book finds access and favor before You to become a carrier of Your glory and Your Kingdom. We declare that everything she has brought forth begins to align with Your perfect will.

We decree that these are the days when mothers arise—mothers of movements, mothers of generations, and mothers of purpose. Just as it is written: "I, Deborah, arose, a mother in Israel" (Judges 5:7).

We declare that every woman finds her place, her territory, and her assignment. She receives favor to rise as a mother—to protect, to nurture, and to establish what You have deposited within her.

Today she rises with authority, walking in her calling, leading generations, and manifesting Your purpose on the earth.

And we declare that through her, this world will see Your latter glory.

In the name of Jesus, Amen.

— Pastor Jorge Valenciano

CHAPTER 10

Mary: Portal of Heaven on Earth

From the beginning, God has sought access to the earth. The original design of humanity included direct communion with heaven, an open relationship where the eternal and the earthly coexisted without barriers. However, after the fall, that access was interrupted. Man was separated from the presence, but God's purpose was not canceled; it simply remained awaiting restoration.

Heaven still desired to manifest on the earth. Even so, there was an unbreakable spiritual principle: the heavenly does not invade the earthly without agreement. God does not break in; God responds to availability. He does not force His will upon man; He seeks a door, a surrender, a life that will say yes.

This principle is not only theological; it is practical and eternal. God has always worked through willing people. Not because He depends on man, but because He decided to include him in His design. Heaven manifests where it finds agreement. And that agreement is not always seen in perfection, but in availability.

When Heaven Seeks Access

In Eden, there was a woman: Eve. She was created with purpose, with identity, and with a perfect design. She had access, she had position, she had communion. However, she did not become a portal. Although she carried design, she did not sustain alignment. And where there is no obedience, there is no access.

Heaven does not only need an available womb; it needs a surrendered will. Eve had the design, but she did not sustain the obedience necessary to become that meeting point between heaven and earth. Her story reveals that purpose is not fulfilled only by capacity, but by alignment with the voice of God.

This teaches us something profound: it is not enough to be called; it is necessary to remain aligned. It is not enough to have access; it is necessary to sustain it. Because heaven does not rest upon potential, but upon obedience.

The Negotiation of Heaven

Centuries later, heaven once again seeks access… and finds a woman.

"Now in the sixth month the angel Gabriel was sent by God… to a virgin betrothed… and the virgin's name was Mary." (Luke 1:26–27)

Heaven did not impose. Heaven announced. The response was not forced; it was awaited.

"And behold, you will conceive in your womb and bring forth a Son… and of His kingdom there will be no end." (Luke 1:31–33)

It was not a forced command, but a divine invitation.

An eternal assignment was being presented to a woman on the earth. Heaven was literally negotiating access, seeking a response that would allow the invisible to become visible.

This reveals the character of God: He does not seek to control, He seeks to collaborate. He does not seek to impose, He seeks agreement. Heaven was waiting for a response that would open the door to manifestation.

But the most important thing was still missing: Mary's decision.

The "Yes" That Opened Heaven

Then Mary answered:

"Behold the maidservant of the Lord! Let it be to me according to your word." (Luke 1:38)

That "yes" was not a simple response. It was total surrender. In that moment, Mary not only accepted a natural process, but she became a meeting point between two dimensions. Heaven found in Mary what it did not find in Eve: a completely surrendered will.

And where there is surrender, there is access.

That "yes" did not only impact her life; it impacted history.

It was a "yes" that carried eternity.

It was a "yes" that opened the way for heaven to descend to earth.

Today, that same principle remains active. God continues to seek women who will say "yes," not from emotion, but from conviction. A "yes" that does not depend on understanding everything, but on trusting the One who spoke it.

Carrier of the Kingdom

Mary carried more than a son in her womb; she carried the Kingdom. Her womb became the place where the eternal took on human form, where the promise became flesh.

"And the Word became flesh and dwelt among us… and we beheld His glory." (John 1:14)

Heaven did not lift man up to reach it. Heaven descended through a woman. It was impossible for humanity to ascend on its own, so God designed an access point: heaven entering the earth through a surrendered womb.

Mary became that access, a living portal where the invisible became visible and the eternal was manifested in the temporal.

And this is not only history; it is a pattern. Because just as God found in Mary an available woman, He continues seeking women today who become portals where His will can manifest on the earth.

Mother of a Movement

Mary was not only the mother of Jesus; she was the mother of a movement. She carried, protected, and gave birth to what would transform entire generations. Her motherhood was not merely biological; it was deeply prophetic.

She sustained within herself the fulfillment of an eternal promise. That is why she is called mother, not only because she gave birth, but because she gave beginning. Because every mother, in God's design, does not only bring life, but introduces purpose into the earth.

And this reveals something powerful: what a woman carries has generational impact. What she sustains in the process becomes legacy in time.

The Highest Level of Maternity

However, there is an even deeper dimension within the design of a woman that must be understood: the highest level of maternity is not only to give birth in the natural, but to give birth in the Spirit.

Giving birth in the natural produces life on earth, but giving birth in the Spirit produces life in eternity.

There are women who have given birth to children physically, yet have never given birth to purpose in the Spirit. And there are others who, even without having given birth naturally, have produced entire generations in the Spirit, raising sons and daughters who walk in the design of God.

This reveals a powerful truth: maternity is not limited to the biological—it is a spiritual function.

To give birth in the Spirit is to carry what God deposits until it takes form in the lives of others. It is to intercede until transformation is seen. It is to sustain processes that are not always visible, but are shaping destiny.

It is to raise spiritual sons and daughters, to form generations, to establish purpose in others, and to become a channel through which heaven continues to multiply on the earth.

The apostle Paul expressed this dimension when he

said:

"My little children, for whom I labor in birth again until Christ is formed in you." (Galatians 4:19)

This was not symbolic language without weight—it was a spiritual reality. He understood that giving birth in the Spirit involves process, involves pain, involves surrender… but it produces something eternal.

And here is the difference:

- The natural has an impact in time, but the spiritual has an impact in eternity. That is why the calling of a woman is not only to give life, but to form purpose.

- Not only to bring children into the world, but to raise sons and daughters for the Kingdom.

- Not only to multiply in the natural, but to establish in the eternal.

When a woman understands this, her perspective shifts. She stops measuring her value by what she produces in the visible, and begins to understand the weight of what she can produce in the invisible.

She becomes a woman who does not only give birth… but forms destiny.

And this is the kind of maternity that transcends generations.

The Design of Woman

When a woman gives birth, she is not receiving; she is giving. We do not say that a woman "receives" a birth, but that she gives birth, because in that act there is surrender, sacrifice, and manifestation.

Woman does not only produce life; she introduces purpose into the world. Every birth is an offering. Every life is an assignment. Woman was designed to be a channel through which what God determines in heaven can be established on the earth.

And in this design, we find dignity, value, and eternal purpose.

The Pain of Giving Birth

Giving birth always involves pain. There is no birth without process, nor manifestation without pressure. The pain of labor is not punishment; it is evidence that something is being formed and is about to manifest.

When a woman enters labor, her body responds to an invisible reality that is about to become visible. There is pressure, there is discomfort, there is sacrifice. However, that pain does not signal the end, but the beginning. It is the sign that what has been conceived is ready to come into the light.

In the same way, in the spiritual realm, every purpose God deposits in a woman goes through a process of gestation. And when the moment comes for it to manifest, there will be pain. There will be pressure. There will be moments when it seems easier to give up than to continue. But that pain is not loss; it is transition.

It is the crossing between the eternal and the natural.

The pain of giving birth is the price of introducing into the earth what heaven has already determined. It is the language of sacrifice, the language of love, the language of someone who is willing to give everything so that the purpose of God may be fulfilled.

But it is important to understand this: pain is not the

destination.

Pain does not define the result. Pain announces that the result is near.

After the pain comes the fruit. After the pressure comes the manifestation. After the process comes the impact. What is born from that place is not temporary; it carries eternal weight and produces an effect in generations.

Just as Mary carried the purpose and went through the process until giving birth to the Savior, every woman who has been called by God will have to go through her own process of spiritual birth. And even though it hurts, that pain will bear fruit, and that fruit will transform the earth.

Spiritual Abortions

Not everything God deposits in a life comes to manifest on the earth. There are purposes that were conceived in moments of encounter with God, words that were received with clarity, and assignments that began with conviction, but at some point in the process were interrupted before seeing their fulfillment. This does not always happen because of lack of capacity, but because of exhaustion in the process, pressure, pain, or not understanding the weight of what was being carried. In the natural, an abortion represents the interruption of a life before its manifestation; in the spiritual, something similar happens when something God deposited is abandoned, rejected, or allowed to die before its time, not because it lacked purpose, but because it was not sustained until the end.

When the Process Is Interrupted

The enemy does not always try to prevent a woman from conceiving purpose, because he knows that God has already planted eternal seeds within her; what he attempts to do is interrupt the process of gestation, wear down her faith, cloud her vision, and make her believe that what she is carrying is not worth the cost or the effort. In this way, he allows conception to happen, but fights intensely against perseverance, knowing that the most powerful thing is not only what God deposits, but what actually comes to birth. It is in the midst of that exhaustion that many women, without realizing it, release what God entrusted to them, not necessarily out of rebellion, but out of weariness, frustration, or the pressure of a process that seemed to have no end.

At that point, the mind begins to justify what the spirit once embraced with faith. What was once conviction becomes doubt, and what was once clarity becomes confusion. Little by little, what was once received with certainty is abandoned. However, the fact that something was interrupted does not mean it never had destiny; it means the process was stopped before its time. And even in that interruption, the purpose does not lose its value before God, because everything He originates carries within itself an eternal intention.

The Call to Repentance

But there is a truth that must be clearly established: God does not reveal these things to condemn, but to restore. The intention of the Holy Spirit is not to expose in order to destroy, but to illuminate in order to correct and realign. If at any point you released what He gave you, if you allowed something that had been planted in your spirit to die, or if you abandoned a process because the pain seemed greater than the promise, today is not a day of guilt, but of return.

Repentance is not remaining in the mistake or living bound to the past; it is returning to the original design, realigning with the voice of God, and taking up again what had been released. It is recognizing that at some point direction was lost, but deciding to return to it with new determination. It is being able to say from the depths of the heart: "Lord, I return to You. I believe again in what You spoke to me. I choose to sustain what You placed in me, even if the process is not easy." Because true repentance does not only change the mind; it changes the direction of life.

God Restores What Was Interrupted

God has the ability to restore what seemed lost and to reactivate what was stopped. He is not limited by past seasons or by decisions made in moments of weakness. What was not born in one season can be formed again in another, and what was interrupted can be restored when there is a genuine willingness to carry it again. Scripture declares:

> *"I will restore to you the years that the swarming locust has eaten..."* (Joel 2:25)

Revealing that heaven does not operate with final endings, but with continuous redemption.

God does not cancel purpose; He keeps it, preserves it, and presents it again when He finds a willing heart. Even what seemed to have been lost does not completely disappear from God's plan, but remains like a seed waiting for the right conditions to germinate again. This reveals the character of God: He is Restorer, Redeemer, and faithful to what He has spoken, even when man has not been faithful to sustain it.

Returning to Carry Purpose Again

Today, more than confrontation, God is extending an invitation. Just as He sought Mary, He continues seeking available women, not perfect, but surrendered; not without history, but with the willingness to say "yes" again. Because a restored "yes" has the power to produce what an abandoned "yes" could not manifest. This is not about starting from zero, but about taking it up again from a place of greater understanding, greater dependence, and a more mature faith.

Returning to carry purpose means accepting the process again, embracing the time of formation, and trusting that what God deposited in the beginning still has destiny. It means walking with the understanding that pain is not a sign of failure, but evidence that something eternal is being formed. And in that moment, the woman stops living from what she lost and begins to walk from what God has decided to restore in her, becoming once again a portal through which heaven can manifest on the earth.

Prayer Of Restoration And Reactivation

Eternal Father, in the name of Jesus, today I come before You recognizing that You have deposited purpose in my life. You have sown eternal things within me, callings and assignments that were born in Your heart. And today, with humility, I recognize that in some moments I did not know how to sustain what You entrusted to me, and I released things that had destiny in You.

Lord, today I repent and return to You. I renounce every lie that made me believe it was too late or that what was lost could not be restored. Today I realign myself with Your voice and say "yes" again to what You spoke over my life.

Holy Spirit, heal my heart and restore in me what was interrupted. Remove all fear, weariness, and doubt, and fill me with faith, clarity, and determination to sustain the process until I see fulfillment.

I declare that what was stopped is reactivated, that what seemed lost is restored, and that I carry purpose again with new strength. I will not release what You entrust to me. I will walk with You and trust in Your timing.

Thank You because You are not finished with me. Your purpose remains active in my life.

In the name of Jesus. Amen.

Called to Give Birth to Purpose

Just as Mary gave birth to Christ, God continues calling women to give birth to His purpose on the earth. Not all will give birth in the same way, but all are called to produce something eternal: purpose, calling, generations, and movements.

Woman was not designed only to receive; she was designed to manifest. She was designed to be a portal.

Many women have waited for the perfect moment to begin, without understanding that purpose does not respond to ideal conditions, but to obedience. God is not looking for women who have everything figured out; He is looking for women who are willing to walk by faith.

Giving birth to purpose will not always be comfortable, but it will always be meaningful. What God deposits in a woman has destiny, has weight, and has impact.

Women Who Give Birth to the Kingdom

God is still looking for women who respond like Mary: "Let it be to me according to your word."

Women who do not resist the process, who do not fear the cost, and who understand that carrying purpose may hurt, but it will always transform generations. The process may be uncomfortable and the timing may feel uncertain, but what is born of God always has destiny.

You were not called only to exist. You were called to give birth to what heaven wants to manifest on the earth. But every portal is tested, and every woman who carries the purpose of God will pass through fire, not to destroy her, but to purify what she carries within.

These are women who understand that their lives do not completely belong to them, but are instruments in the hands of God. Women who do not negotiate their process, who do not retreat under pressure, and who understand that what they carry has eternal purpose.

Keys to Remember

- God seeks availability, not perfection
- A "yes" opens access to heaven
- Purpose must be sustained until it manifests
- God restores what was interrupted

Prophetic Declaration

Today I declare over your life that you become a portal for the purpose of God on the earth. I declare that your spiritual womb is activated to give birth to the eternal. I declare that you have the courage to say "yes" to heaven, even when you do not fully understand the process.

I declare that what God deposited in you will not be stopped, but manifested in His perfect time. You rise as a woman who carries, protects, and gives birth to the purpose of God.

In the name of Jesus. Amen.

Prayer

Beloved Father,

Today I lift my voice before You for every woman who has journeyed through these pages, declaring that none of them have walked through the fire in vain. I declare that every process, every trial, and every moment of pressure has been used by You to form, establish, and reveal the eternal purpose You placed within them.

"That the genuineness of your faith, being much more precious than gold that perishes, though it is tested by fire, may be found to praise, honor, and glory at the revelation of Jesus Christ" (1 Peter 1:7).

I declare that the fire did not destroy them—it refined them. It did not weaken them—it strengthened them. Today they rise with a purified faith, with a firm identity, and with a spiritual authority established in You.

I prophesy that they are entering a new season where they no longer walk from their wounds, but from purpose; no longer react from pain, but govern from Your presence. They rise as women who are fireproof—steadfast, mature, and aligned with the design of heaven.

I declare that their generations will be marked by their faithfulness, that their homes will be established in righteousness, and that their lives will become living evidence of Your glory on the earth.

Today they receive the strength to remain, the clarity to advance, and the authority to establish what You have ordained.

In the name of Jesus, Amen.

— Prophet Naomi Espinoza

Fireproof

The fire did not come to destroy you—it came to reveal you. Throughout these pages, we have walked through the original design, the pain of the fall, the restoration of identity, the vision of the Kingdom, intercession, and maturity. Each chapter has been a part of the process, but everything converges at one point: the fire.

Fire is uncomfortable. Fire purifies. Fire reveals what is gold and what is not. Not everything that enters the fire remains, but everything that remains after the fire has been refined.

"…that the genuineness of your faith… may be found to praise, honor, and glory…" (1 Peter 1:7)

God does not waste the fire. He uses it with intention. What many see as destruction, God uses for formation. What appears to be the end is, in reality, the process where He separates what is temporary from what is eternal.

The Fire That Forms

Perhaps you have walked through abandonment, rejection, betrayal, loss, or silent battles that no one else saw. Moments where pain seemed stronger than hope, and where the process felt endless. Yet the fire was not your end—it was your process.

What the enemy tried to use to break you, God used to form you. In the midst of the fire, your true strength was revealed—but even more importantly, your dependence on God was revealed. Because fire has the ability to strip away everything you once relied on, until all that remains is the One who never fails.

And in that place, you came to understand that your identity was not in what you lost, but in the One who called you.

The Woman Who Remains

A fireproof woman is not perfect—she is persevering. She is not the one who never fell, but the one who learned how to rise. She is not the one who never cried, but the one who turned her tears into intercession.

She has understood something that transforms the way she lives: her story does not end in the wound—it ends in purpose. Pain does not define her destiny; it prepares her. Circumstances do not determine her identity; they reveal what God already placed within her.

Generations Marked by Your Fire

Your process was never only about you. Your children will see your faith. Your generations will walk in the inheritance you defended in prayer. Even if today you cannot yet see the full result, what you sowed in tears will be reaped in victory.

"Those who sow in tears shall reap in joy." (Psalm 126:5)

The fire did not only transform you—it transformed what comes after you. Every prayer, every decision to remain, every moment you chose to trust God instead of giving up left a mark that will reach generations.

Your struggle was not invisible. Your faithfulness was not overlooked. God saw every moment, every surrender, every act of obedience.

Your Place Is Established

You were not born to survive—you were born to establish. You were not created to react to what happens around you—you were created to govern from the presence. You were not made to live intimidated by the process—you were made to walk in spiritual authority.

God is not finished with you. There is still vision. There is still purpose. There are still generations waiting for your voice, your example, and your obedience.

Marks of a Fireproof Woman

A fireproof woman is not recognized by what she avoids, but by what she sustains. Her life reflects a strength that does not come from her circumstances, but from her relationship with God.

She remains firm when everything around her is unstable. She does not negotiate her identity for approval, because she knows who she is in God. She learns to depend on the Lord rather than her emotions, and even when she is wounded, she chooses to respond from maturity rather than from pain.

She perseveres in prayer even when she does not see immediate results. She walks in obedience even when she does not fully understand the process. She guards her heart even after being hurt, because she knows that becoming hardened will not protect her—it will disconnect her from purpose.

She does not abandon the process—she walks through it. She does not stop believing, even when it would be easier to give up. Because she understands that the fire is not her enemy—it is the tool God uses to form her.

A fireproof woman is not the one who avoids trials, but the one who is not broken by them. The fire does not consume her—it defines her.

Final Commission

This book does not end—it sends you.

It sends you to rise, to walk, to pray, to build, and to govern from the presence. It sends you to become the woman the fire could not destroy, the woman the process could not break, the woman who remains when everything tried to stop her.

You were not formed to go backward. You were formed to advance, to establish, and to manifest the purpose of God on the earth.

Keys to Remember

- The fire is not the end—it is the process
- Your story does not end in the wound
- You were formed, not destroyed
- Your purpose remains active

Final Prophetic Declaration

Today I declare over your life that the fire did not define you—it refined you. I declare that your identity is established in Christ, and no one can remove it. I declare that your home will stand firm, your generations will be blessed, and your legacy will be visible on the earth.

I declare that you walk in spiritual authority, in maturity, and in eternal purpose. What began as a trial ends as a testimony.

- You are a restored woman.
- You are a strengthened woman.
- You are a fireproof woman.

In the name of Jesus, Amen.

This is not the end of your story…

it is the beginning of your manifestation.

Author's Letter

Dear woman,

If this book has found its way into your hands, it is not by accident. I passionately believe that God allows divine encounters at the precise moments of our lives.

Perhaps you are reading these words in the middle of a trial. Perhaps you are coming out of a battle. Or maybe you are just beginning to discover who you are in God. Whatever season you are in, I want you to know this: you are not alone.

I, too, have walked through processes. I have faced the fire. I have had to learn how to remain when everything around me seemed to be shifting beneath my feet. And in every stage, God showed me that the fire did not come to destroy me—it came to form me.

Being a woman is not weakness—it is design. Being a mother is not limitation—it is legacy. Being an intercessor is not a burden—it is authority.

God has never made a mistake with you. Your story is not an accident. Your process is not in vain.

If you have ever doubted your worth, return to the origin. If you have ever lost your voice, return to His presence. If you have ever felt small, remember that heaven calls you daughter.

Do not allow your past to define your future. Do not allow wounds to silence your purpose. Do not allow the fire to make you retreat when it was sent to propel you forward.

My prayer is that these pages have not only informed you, but transformed you. That they have not only taught you, but activated you.

Rise with identity. Walk in maturity. Intercede with

authority. Love deeply. Build generations.

The world needs women who are steadfast, filled with the Spirit, aligned with heaven, and established in their purpose.

And I believe you are one of them.

With love and hope,

Prophet Naomi Espinoza

The Prayers of a Mother

A mother's intercession is not weak—it is persistent. It is firm. It is constant.

Jesus told the parable of the persistent widow to teach us that persevering prayer produces justice:

> *"There was in a certain city a judge who did not fear God nor regard man. Now there was a widow in that city; and she came to him, saying, 'Get justice for me from my adversary'… Yet because this widow troubles me I will avenge her…" (Luke 18:2–5)*

A mother does not pray once—she prays until she sees fulfillment.

A mother's prayer protects, restores, and raises generations. This chapter contains prayers to declare over the family, the woman, the nation, and future generations—not from fear, but from faith.

Prayer for the Family

"Get justice for me from my adversary." (Luke 18:3)

Heavenly Father, in the name of Jesus, I cover my family with the precious blood of Christ. I declare that my household belongs to the Lord, and that no plan of the enemy will prosper against it.

I raise spiritual protection around my home. I declare that Your presence dwells in our house and that Your peace governs our decisions.

In the name of Jesus, I restore everything that has been stolen. What was attacked will be strengthened. What was wounded will be healed. What was scattered will be gathered.

My generations will serve You. My home will be filled with Your anointing. Your favor will follow my children and my children's children.

In the name of Jesus, Amen.

Activate Your Prayer

Write the names of your children or family members you are interceding for:

____

____

____

____

What biblical promise are you believing for your household?

____

____

____

____

What specific situation are you presenting before God today?

____

____

____

____

Prayer for the Woman

"I arose as a mother in Israel." (Judges 5:7)

Lord, raise up women who are firm and passionate for Your presence. Women who do not live distracted, but aligned with Your purpose.

Awaken a generation of women who intercede for their cities, who cry out for transformation, and who walk with spiritual boldness.

Raise up women like Deborah—women who hear Your voice, who act with determination, and who proclaim hope and restoration over their surroundings.

I declare that women rise in spiritual authority, not out of pride, but out of obedience.

In the name of Jesus, Amen.

Activate Your Declaration

In what area do you need to rise with spiritual boldness?

____

____

____

____

What city, community, or family are you called to cover in prayer?

____

____

____

____

Prayer for Women in Authority

"Go, gather all the Jews… If I perish, I perish." (Esther 4:16)

Father, we pray for every woman who holds a position of leadership—in the church, in the family, in education, in government, and in society.

Just as Esther was positioned for a specific time, we declare that every woman in authority will understand her assignment and walk in courage.

May they intercede for their nation. May they make decisions with the fear of God. May they act with wisdom and justice.

Lord, bring healing to our land. Raise up women who lead with integrity and a pure heart.

In the name of Jesus, Amen.

Activate Your Intercession

Write the name of a woman leader you are praying for:

____

____

____

What are you believing God will do in your nation?

____

____

____

Prayer for the Womb and Generations

"Rahab and her family dwelt in Israel…" (Joshua 6:25)

Heavenly Father, we declare spiritual fruitfulness and purpose over every woman.

Just as the earth was designed to produce fruit, we declare that every woman will bear fruit in her time—whether through biological children or spiritual children.

I declare that wombs are fertile ground. I declare that the generations that arise will walk in obedience, leadership, and the fear of God.

I declare that our children will be firm in identity, filled with the Holy Spirit, and established in purpose.

What begins today in prayer will be seen tomorrow in fulfillment.

In the name of Jesus, Amen.

Activate Your Faith

Write the names of the generations you are covering:

What spiritual legacy do you desire to leave?

Closing of the Chapter

A mother's prayer does not end when she says "Amen." It continues in faith, in perseverance, and in expectation.

Heaven responds when a woman rises in intercession.

Without warfare, there is no victory. Without prayer, there is no manifestation.

But when a mother prays… generations are changed.

Connect with Naomi Espinoza

Stay connected for messages, teachings, and updates. Scan the code or follow the platforms below.

 @PROPHETNAOMIESPINOZA

 PROPHET NAOMI ESPINOZA